•SOLILOQUIES & EPIPHANIES•

·SOLILOQUIES & EPIPHANIES·

·SOLILOQUIES & EPIPHANIES·

al'vina janae

•SOLILOQUIES & EPIPHANIES•

Soliloquies & Epiphanies

Copyright © 2018 by Al'vina Artis
All rights reserved. Printed in the United States of America.
No part of this book may be used or reproduced in any manner whatsoever
without written permission from the author except in the case of brief
quotations.

ISBN: 1718945655
ISBN-13: 978-1718945654

·SOLILOQUIES & EPIPHANIES·

·SOLILOQUIES & EPIPHANIES·

...

for the broken the fallen and the hopeless
know that there is life after death

...

·SOLILOQUIES & EPIPHANIES·

· Chapters ·

Descension 9

Transition 83

Ascension 121

·SOLILOQUIES & EPIPHANIES·

• DESCENSION •

•SOLILOQUIES & EPIPHANIES•

Soliloquies Wasted

I am *wasting* my breath with each word that I utter unto you in an attempt to get you to understand me. Every sentence I speak seems to be a **nuisance** around your neck as if my pain is too much of a burden for you to bear. I've sacrificed so much to be with you. I've pushed aside my life long dreams, but you can't find the time to take heed to my pleas. I am down on my knees begging you to love me, but my cries don't seem to reach your ears. *You don't hear me* when I'm screaming from the bottom of my soul. I asked you not to let me go and you walked away so easily. We were seamlessly entwined but now I am hanging on by a thread. My *voice* has gotten **lost** in the echoes of your head. I've faded into the shadows of a heart that no longer beats. I'm the forgotten memory of a love that used to be. I tried to plead my case when our souls were face to face but you chose not to comprehend, and I can't prevent our end when you yourself are the source of our descent...

Impatient

I'm growing impatient
of waiting for you to love me
of waiting for you to want me
I know I deserve more
I know that I'm **worth** more
but my heart has already spoken
the *thought* of what we could be
is so beautiful to me
but time is slipping away
and I'm afraid that I may
have to do the same

•SOLILOQUIES & EPIPHANIES•

<u>Center Stage</u>

I will not **fade to black** in your background
simply because your foreground in preoccupied
I cannot sit idly behind the curtains
I have to be seen
I'm not asking to be in the spotlight at all times
but I need a *permanent* spot on your stage

·SOLILOQUIES & EPIPHANIES·

Love by Numbers

it's not enough, loving you in *30*-minute increments
hugging you **once** every *7* days
you stay *2.6* miles away
but it feels as if you're on another continent
1 hour in your car, then we're quickly torn apart
2 hours in your bed, then the love goes dead
now I'm forced to spend my nights alone
hoping to hear your voice
on the other end of my phone
even if it's only *5* minutes
it'll lift my spirits
to hear you tell me that you miss me
to hear you tell me how badly
you want to kiss me
you get me in ways that no other man can
and my heart fits so perfectly
in the palm of your *2* hands
but you've got your fists clenched
so, I keep my love at bay
because it's not enough, loving you **once** every *7* days

·SOLILOQUIES & EPIPHANIES·

even when I'm right in front of you
with my body pressed against yours
you still don't see me
at least not the real me
and it kills me
to be in your presence
when your **mind**
is no longer present

-blind

Lost in the Unknown

once I began to wonder *if* you loved me
I realized you possessed no love for me
if you did, I would have known
it would have shown
it would have been *written on your skin* – and mine
as if we bathed in each other's souls
but here I am
naked and **alone**
in the cold
wondering if you love me

·SOLILOQUIES & EPIPHANIES·

...

my blood on your hands
your tears on my skin
our love reached its *end*
but still, we *pretend*
to be **more than just friends**
as if *lust* could ever *mend*
this tapestry of deceit
that caused us to descend

...

Denial

we keep *pretending* that we aren't **broken**
as if **lies** could *fix* us
placing band aids on severed limbs
as if **denial** could *heal* us

·SOLILOQUIES & EPIPHANIES·

selig

I was not ready to lose you
I was not ready to live without you
I was not ready to be completely and so abruptly
torn apart from you
you dropped into my life
like an angel formed just for me
then you turned and walked away
and left me mourning on bloody knees
if it were up to me
we would have **never** met our end
you would have **never** left my side
our souls would still be entwined
if it were up to me
we would have made love
and created life
and it would be **our** child who's keeping you up at night
not hers
now I'm dwelling on my pain
wondering what it's worth
to have known and loved you
was both a blessing and a curse
you made my heart grow in size
then you watched me as I died
your love sparkled in my eyes
but it was **you** who made me cry
and it was you who let me drown
it was you who pushed me down
with those same hands
that once caressed my face when I'd frown

but still, I crave your kiss
I miss our moments of bliss
in your arms is where I realized
soulmates truly exist
but you gave your soul to her
the moment you laid in bed with her
now you are forever bound to her
as I am forever doomed to hurt

...

•SOLILOQUIES & EPIPHANIES•

Stranded

like waves abandoning the sand
you held out your hand
with no intentions of ever truly loving me

did you plan this?

did you purposely reel me in
just to leave me **stranded?**

love was nothing, but a four letter **lie** that slipped from your lips but for some reason, I still *believed* you when you said it.

<u>-*love lies*</u>

·SOLILOQUIES & EPIPHANIES·

...

tell me you've found another
tell me she's treating you better
tell me how she's doing everything

that I didn't

tell me, so I can't **stop wondering** what I should have done
different

...

•SOLILOQUIES & EPIPHANIES•

Reminiscing

right now, I want to call you
I want to pour out my heart to you
and tell you how much I hate being apart from you
I miss your skin
I *miss how we sinned*
I miss how free I felt when I let you in
chest to chest
nose to nose
breathing in each other's **souls**
the car was in park but
you drove me out of control
you drove me insane
and I relished in the pain
for a while but
without the pleasure it just doesn't feel the same
I'm *hurting*, and I need you to **heal me**
I'm *empty*, and I need you to **fill me**
can you feel me – drifting away
reel me in, I want so badly to stay – afloat
but I'm drowning while you're swimming away
salt water burns my lungs as I call out your name
I want to call you
I want to pour out my heart to you
and tell you how much I hate being apart from you

so, *I call you*

prepared to spill my guts

the phone stops ringing

but you don't pick up...

·SOLILOQUIES & EPIPHANIES·

<u>Fading Rainbows</u>

I thought I knew what colors were
until you opened my eyes to
secret pigments and hidden hues

then just like a **rainbow**

you *faded* away too

The Last Time

I just want to see you one last time
hear your voice one last time
feel your warmth
watch you smile
be eye to eye
one last time
if I'd known our Sun would no longer rise
if I'd known our light would cease to shine
if I'd known our *love* was beginning to **die**
I would have kissed you longer than I did
                              the last time

•SOLILOQUIES & EPIPHANIES•

<u>Oxygen i</u>

I cannot *breathe* when I'm with you
but I *suffocate* every time you **leave**

when I *reminisce* on the way I used to feel when we'd touch

I'm no longer tough enough to live without your love

my knees go weak and I find myself *falling* for you **again**

with just enough **strength** to *crawl back* into your hands.

-relapse

•SOLILOQUIES & EPIPHANIES•

Sacrificial Inspiration

I used you as fuel for my fire
but I'm the one who got burned
like a dog returning to its vomit
repeating my folly
I keep running back to you
reopening old wounds
its like *I can't thrive without pain*
like I can't write unless **your name**
is on the tip of my tongue
choking me
holding me hostage
yes, I'm dying to break free
but once I'm liberated
back in your chains is where I wish to be
you *bruise me* so **beautifully**
and your *kisses* taste of **cruelty**
and the stories you *inspire*
makes me love the painful things you do to me
so, I'm **sacrificing my heart**
for the sake of the art
I let you kill me again and again
just so I can *bleed* more ink into my *pen*

•SOLILOQUIES & EPIPHANIES•

...

you ran away with *my heart* trapped inside **your chest**
and left me struggling to live on within this hollowed flesh

...

·SOLILOQUIES & EPIPHANIES·

how many times can I die and come back
I don't even recognize my own heart beat anymore
my bones don't feel like they are my own
and I'm not sure if this skin belongs to me
I've **lost myself** in men who claimed to love me
but all they did was use me
and abuse me
and take the parts of me that they liked most
they took everything I had
everything I was
and left me with a *deformed soul*
and a **foreign body**

-plundered

I'm afraid that I've given so much of myself
to men who didn't *deserve* me
that I won't have enough left
for the man who is truly **worthy**

-empty

Holding On i

I know it's senseless for me to crave you the way I do
but my heart has wants and needs
my soul is yearning for affection
that I know you **can't** give me
and that should be enough to push me away
but instead, I'm living out my life with you
in **hopes** that things will change
holding on to all the sweet parts
because the good outweighs the bad
even though the bad is painful
even though your love is fatal
and sometimes hateful
I still remain faithful – how *stupid* of me
I'm still refusing to leave
even when the tables take a turn for the worst
and I feel as though I can no longer handle the hurt

Holding On ii

I find myself being faithful to you
picturing a future with you
when in all actuality
I'm not sure if I'm the woman God chose for you
or if you're the man He chose for me
it's ironic to me that He would preordain my heart
to someone who could **never** love it completely
you give me pieces of you
and I make do with what I can
so it's *unfair* for you to have my whole soul
within your hands
but still, I offer you all of me
in *hopes* that we could someday be
everything I've dreamed of
but my imagination is clouded
my heart and mind both doubting
every word you say
you tell me things will soon change
and that it won't always be this way
but I can't see us getting better
and I can't hide my pain forever

they always say "the truth shall set you free"
but what if I don't want to be free
the *lies* are what keeps us **chained** together
and I love being *trapped* with you

-stockholm syndrome

•SOLILOQUIES & EPIPHANIES•

Barriers

your fingers have traced
barriers around my heart
that no one else can seem to cross
I am lost in our love
and my soul feels so at peace
when it's just us two
but what am I to do
if I suddenly need someone
to save me from **you**?

•SOLILOQUIES & EPIPHANIES•

...

it's not that I couldn't see the signs
I just didn't want to
so, I *chose* not to
your heart went *numb*
and I played **dumb**
because I felt better receiving *fake love*
than I did receiving **none**

...

Trussed by Trust

your love was a *noose* around my neck and I cut the rope, but my fingertips are still bloody from picking at the pieces of pain that still manage to **choke** me.

there's so much I want to say
but my lips are in *chains*
my tongue has become a *slave*
to **yesterday's pain**
I cannot speak from my heart
for my soul has been torn apart
the very moment my thoughts start
I find myself *blinded* by the **dark**

-tongue tied

Set Me Free

I cannot continue to live this way
there are too many burdens
bearing down on my soul
taking a toll on who I am
this isn't me
God please **set me free**
let me float away with the rain
let the droplets *cleanse* my pain
let me be *reborn* again
with *no memory* of **past** shame

•SOLILOQUIES & EPIPHANIES•

it's disgraceful how we only run
back to God after the very thing
that led us *astray* begins to cause
too much **pain**

-backsliding

...

there's a fine line between *moving on* and **giving up** and I'm still trying to figure out where upon that precipice does my heart and soul stand.

...

<u>*Goodbye*</u>

it hurts my soul to walk away from you
so, I'll have to stay away from you
because you will **never** be completely mine
and I cannot endure the pain of another
temporary goodbye

Silent Killer

they say that I dodged a *bullet*
but they don't see the leaking holes in my heart
they don't see the missing pieces of my soul
they can't feel the freezing cold in my bones
my body still yearns for you
my veins are screaming for you
my lungs cannot breathe
I'm down on my knees
I've been torn in two
and they don't have a clue
they say that I dodged a bullet
but they don't know I'm *bleeding out* anyway
because they can't see the **knife** you left in my back

Casualty of Love

remember when we told each other
we would *always* be together
even if we decided to give our hearts
to someone on the outside
the bond that we forged on the inside
was supposed to keep us entwined
but you cut ties and burned bridges
you set our friendship on fire
while I was still in it
you left me screaming for your love
banging on the windows of your soul
as you watched from the other side – unfazed
so, I had to save myself
because if I'd waited on your help
I surely would have died
I think I did die – on the inside
I met death face to face
my tears fell for 40 days
I drowned in my sorrows
I couldn't recognize tomorrow
I wept as I slept, and my pillows are still wet
my pillows are still stained
with mascara that I wore for you on our last date
the very last day that your face graced my space
before you snatched your love away
like a thief in the night
I went to sleep in love
and woke up with your knife in my back

·SOLILOQUIES & EPIPHANIES·

I'm cracked open and weeping
my heart – barely beating
you could've at least looked me in my eyes as you killed me
now here we are months later
and I'm the one feeling guilty
I'm the one feeling stressed
because you're pressed to be friends
and you want to make amends
for leaving me alone to rewrite how we'd end
but I don't want to let you in
so you can hurt me *again*
I know I promised I'd stay
and I mean everything I say
but you threw our love away
when you chose to walk away
and yet, those words still linger in my mind
like goosebumps left behind
as your fingers traced my spine...

but that's all in the past
we knew our love wouldn't last
we fell too hard and too fast
so we were destined to crash
I just didn't know that I'd crash all *alone*
while you ran from the damage
leaving me to heal on my own

...

Undone

does your heart not quiver as I'm miles away crying?
miles away **dying** – *on the inside*
I thought our souls had become one
do you not feel that *half of you* has come **undone?**

Final Act

I don't have the energy to continue smiling while I'm *dying* on the **inside**. I can feel my *mask* cracking; I can feel the **pain**
                                      hacking its way out

Secrets & Lies

I'm **afraid** to show you the *real* me
I've got secrets lurking
just below the surface of my skin
so that's why I can't let you in
or let you get too close
because then you'll know
you'll find what I've been hiding
you'll realize that I've been lying
and the things that you'll discover
could make you run and duck for cover
or make you leave my side forever
so that's why I have these secrets
that I hardly ever share
and I know that's it's unfair
but I'm just too scared to tell you
too scared to lose you

I Lost You

I stood right in front of you
screaming
crying
bleeding
dying
trying to get you to see me
and not the me you thought I should be
not the pretty me
not the happy me
not the me I'd been *pretending* to be
but the **real me**
with my real pain
and my real scars
and my real screams
that could be heard from afar
I was *vulnerable,* and I was *broken*
and I thought you loved me enough to heal me
or at least enough to try
but the moment I showed you my true self
was the moment your love died

•SOLILOQUIES & EPIPHANIES•

...

you listened to me as I poured out my heart
you **promised** to heal all my broken parts
did it make you feel grand
did you feel like more of a man
being able to take a stand
and save a "damsel in distress"
but in all actuality, **you** were the mess
your soul was alone, dying slowly in the cold
so, I **vowed** to rebuild you – bone by bone
I gave you my heart
when yours could no longer beat
then *you forgot about me*
once you gained enough strength
to stand on your own feet

...

don't make promises to a poet
because words are all they know
and your **lies** will line their soul
as if they are written in stone
and that pain will *stain* their skin
even when the love ends
because *vows* aren't meant for people
who are simply playing **pretend**

-*a poet's pain*

•SOLILOQUIES & EPIPHANIES•

...

I hope the *guilt* eats you alive
it's your turn to **die** inside

...

Maybe...

maybe if I dressed myself in your flesh
maybe if I swallowed your voice
maybe if I spoke your thoughts
maybe if I slowly became you

you could finally learn to love me...

•SOLILOQUIES & EPIPHANIES•

...

I made the mistake of
putting you on a *pedestal*
when that spot belonged to me
I gave away my throne
and left myself without a seat
I put you first
I loved you more
I gave you all of me
and now my heart is **shattered**
and I can't find a single piece

...

...

were you not aware that your heart
was still bare beforehand
before you asked for my hand
did you not feel your pain **pulling** you away
as you pushed yourself into my arms
you say you're too broken to love me
you say you fell apart long ago
yet for some reason, you still planted a seed
and you let that seed grow
and you let that seed blossom until I was consumed
with thoughts of creating a life with you
then you *uprooted* the love that you placed in my heart
and left me more **barren** than I was at the start

...

SOLILOQUIES & EPIPHANIES

How?

how do you pick yourself back up
after *falling* from what seemed to be **heaven**?

        how do you piece yourself back together
        when you've **shattered** beyond repair?

how do you learn to love yourself again
when you no longer *recognize* your reflection?

        how do you *rediscover* joy when the person you
        placed your happiness in, runs away with your smile?

how do you begin to live on
when your *lifeline* is **gone**?

•SOLILOQUIES & EPIPHANIES•

why would you let me *fall* for you if you had no intentions of **catching** me? why would you let me carve out my heart and give it to you, if you **never** planned to take care of it?

-cruel intentions

•SOLILOQUIES & EPIPHANIES•

<u>*Death Comes in Three's*</u>

you were my best friend and my greatest love
losing you felt like losing *two* souls at *once*

or **three** if you count my own soul coming undone

•SOLILOQUIES & EPIPHANIES•

my blood is *boiling*
my eyes are *burning*
my tears turn to steam
as they stream down my cheeks
you've lit a fire within me
and not one that brings comfort
these flames in my soul
are raging beyond my control
and they will not stop
until I've melted away the parts of you
that still **fester** inside of me

<u>-hell is a woman</u>

·SOLILOQUIES & EPIPHANIES·

Questioning My Heart

if I ever saw your face again
I don't know what I would do
I'm not sure of which **emotions**
I have left over for you

is it *anger*?

is it *pain*?

do I still *love* you the same?

or am I still harboring *hate*
from when you **massacred** our fate?

•SOLILOQUIES & EPIPHANIES•

...

my cup ran over
my cistern overflowed
my heart poured out *love* just for you

but your thirst was being **quenched** *elsewhere*

...

•SOLILOQUIES & EPIPHANIES•

> I am *drained*
> like an abandoned pool
> I was a fool
> to give my love to you
> but I was lost
> and **you** found me
> then you broke my heart
> and *drowned* me
>
> <u>-a watery grave</u>

...

you ripped your soul away from mine
like a band-aid torn from tender flesh
and left me bleeding and weeping for you
left me open and broken and hoping
for you to return to me
to heal me
to mend my wounded heart
with those very same hands that tore it apart

...

you could've told me you weren't ready
you could've told me you weren't over her
you could've told me you were still in love with her
I would've understood if you were still broken
we both came into this relationship with *bruises and baggage*
but we promised to *help each other heal*
we promised to help each other move on
to help each other breathe again
and love again
but you were only concerned with your own well being
you only cared about healing your own heart
you took everything I had left
you used me to patch your wounds
then you walked away
as I crumbled away

-collateral damage

Incomplete

I've been trying to complete myself with *scattered pieces* of a man who is too hurt to clasp my hand

now I'm wondering **who I am**; *who have I become*

how did I let a *broken soul* force my heart to come **undone?**

Insecure

my mother has always told me that I'm pretty
part of me wants to believe her
but the other part feels that her compliments
are simply a maternal obligation
so, I seek *validation* from men who don't love me
from men who only want one thing from me
they admire my lips, hoping to caress my hips
they speak of beauty in my eyes
when the only thing on their minds
is what's between my thighs
but still, I'm *flattered*
their opinions shouldn't matter
but it makes me feel whole
until I'm **alone**
with no one to console me
so, I call the guy who broke me
asking him to come hold me
and *mold me* into what he needs me to be
in hopes that a **new me**
will make him never want to leave – *again*
but once he's finished, he leaves – **again**

Self-Inflicted

I **punish** *myself* for the pain that I've brought upon myself but hating me only hurts me more so, when does the healing begin?

<u>Hurricanes</u>

I want so badly to be my own *peace*, but I've got too much **pain** brewing inside of me to ever be a *gentle breeze*

Corinthians' Con

love suffers long, but I tend to **run away**
at the first sign of trouble

love is kind, but my heart has **not** lived up
to all that it could be

love does not envy, yet my soul turns **green** whenever
you're in the presence of anyone who is not me

love does not parade itself, yet I'm constantly wishing you
would **proclaim** your feelings from the highest mountain
just so I can know for sure that what we have is **real**

love is not puffed up, yet my head is so **full** with my own
emotions that I **never** take yours into consideration

love does not behave rudely, but I **cut you down** with my
words the very moment something doesn't go my way

love does not seek its own, but I am **selfish** and I'm **entitled**
and I want you all to myself; I want you to **choose me** and
fulfill my needs because my **own** heart is all that matters

love is not provoked, yet I find flames **raging** deep within
whenever your **insolence** seeps beneath my skin

love thinks no evil, but my mind has **not** been the purest
and my eyes have envisioned scenes that I won't ever dare
to speak of

•SOLILOQUIES & EPIPHANIES•

love does not rejoice in iniquity, yet I find **joy** every time we **sin**; skin against skin, I'm only **happy** when I let you in

love rejoices in the truth, but I prefer for you to **lie** to me and tell me only what **I want to hear**

love bears all things, but I **drop** every **burden** that becomes too **heavy** for me

love believes all things, but I **cannot** trust your heart when you say you love me too because that phrase **never** seems true when it's coming from you

love hopes all things, but I've **lost faith** in what we could be

love endures all things, but I don't have the **strength** to carry you in my soul any longer

love never fails, but I **falter** every time

because I let a **broken** man into my heart too many times now I'm left doing time for a crime I didn't commit and I've been *hurt* so many times, I'll probably **never** love again

...

Reflections

I'm looking at pictures of the *old me*
jealous of the girl staring back at me
she doesn't know my **pain**
her heart hasn't been broken
her soul hasn't been shattered
she smiles so genuine and bright
her eyes are dancing with life
I miss her
I *envy* her
but more than anything
I **pity** her
because she doesn't know about the *darkness*
that she will soon become **lost** in

•SOLILOQUIES & EPIPHANIES•

Trust Issues

I can't trust *myself*...

I can't count on my own heart
to pick apart the lies

I can't rely on my own eyes
to show me the truth

so how could I trust **you**?

those hands
those light brown hands
those hands that are rough when they need to be
and soft when they're touching me
those hands that made my body sing
are the same hands that *crushed* my heart
and cause my greatest **pain**

-callused

did you ever really love me
or did you *use me* to fill a **void**
you toyed with my heart
until the one you truly wanted
decided to play her part

-rebound

...

my heart is not a *stepping stone* to lead you away from your pain. you cannot love me just to **spite** the one who hurt you.

...

•SOLILOQUIES & EPIPHANIES•

...

my soul is too honest, and my heart is too pure
to be continuously broken without *consequence* or *recompense*
your **karma** is coming, and you deserve every bit of pain.

...

...

I've never *hated* anyone
until I fell in **love** with you

...

•SOLILOQUIES & EPIPHANIES•

...

after my last heartbreak, I thought I'd be *exempt* from this type of pain; as if being **broken** and **bruised** and **torn** in two would offer me some sort of *immunity*. but I was wrong...

...

•SOLILOQUIES & EPIPHANIES•

...

I read the poems I wrote for him
after you broke my heart
and the words still feel the same
even when I use your name
funny how I thought
I'd never face this pain again
yet here I am
being **broken** by *similar men*
wondering if this **cycle** of sadness
will ever end

...

•SOLILOQUIES & EPIPHANIES•

<u>*Before*</u>

let's go *back to the beginning*

before you became
my **one and only** need

before my lungs required
your breath to *breathe*

back to when my heart
danced to its *own* beat

let's start over and plan
for our paths to **never** meet

•SOLILOQUIES & EPIPHANIES•

•SOLILOQUIES & EPIPHANIES•

• *TRANSITION* •

•SOLILOQUIES & EPIPHANIES•

•SOLILOQUIES & EPIPHANIES•

<u>Cognitive Dissonance</u>

your face is slowly fading from my memories
your voice is no longer the song that loops in my reveries
I'm *afraid* that I am starting to *forget* you
I'm afraid that I am not prepared
to know the taste of freedom
I've been bound by your ghost for so long
constantly holding on to what we **used to be**
your **burden** had become a part of me
but something within me has been chipping away
at the *weight* of your love
unlocking your chains
destroying the reign that you've held over me
but who am I supposed to be
once I'm completely set *free*
my bones do not know how to stand on their *own*
my flesh is not accustomed to harboring only **one** soul...

I cannot **force** my heart to heal; I must let it beat on its *own*. I've planted seeds within my soul, now I'm praying for a miracle.

-let it flow

•SOLILOQUIES & EPIPHANIES•

...

I have no regrets
I did everything right
I loved you more than enough
maybe a little too much
I gave you a thousand second chances
I was there when you needed me
I wiped your tears
I nursed your wounds
I wore your baggage like my favorite purse
I diminished my own worth
so we could be us
but none of that was enough
"it's not you, it's me"
that's probably the only truth you've ever told
because looking back
I can honestly say *I gave it my all*
I gave **you** my all
but we didn't work
because you wouldn't let us
you severed our forever
before we ever had a chance
to truly be together

...

Is There More?

I'm growing tired of writing about pain
and writing about love, or the lack there of
I know there's *more* to life than this
I know there's **more** in my mind than this
but I've been broken and I'm only hoping to heal
I'm just a soul who lost love
but still remembers how it feels

•SOLILOQUIES & EPIPHANIES•

...

I think you really did love me
I think you truly did care
at least I hope you did
because feelings like that
don't fade away overnight
what we had was *right*
what we had was *real* – **to me**
but I think you got scared
at least that's what I tell myself
that's my way of coping
because hating you isn't healthy
so, no I don't blame you
for walking away
you're only human
so you're bound to make mistakes

just know that *leaving me* is the **greatest error**
you will ever make

...

•SOLILOQUIES & EPIPHANIES•

Relief

I was **relieved** when you walked away
you left with all the *baggage* I once considered carrying
I was willing to compromise my dreams
because I thought what we had was real
I was willing to be a mother to your child
I was willing to settle for third place in your heart
because at least there was a spot for me
I knew I deserved more
but I convinced myself that God had other plans for me
a different plan than what I had in mind
and I was willing to walk that line
because I loved having you by my side
but when the going got tough
and the time we spent together wasn't enough
you gathered up your stuff
and walked out of my life
I saw our end coming
I saw what we were becoming
but you and your *false hope* made it all seem okay
you knew exactly what to say
to keep me from running away
because you wanted to be the one to end it
did it make you feel strong to completely break my spirit
to take my heart and crack it
then act like nothing ever happened
you turned my sunshine into rain
then you ignored me and my pain
I cried that entire day

·SOLILOQUIES & EPIPHANIES·

for twenty-four hours straight
but those *tears* **cleansed** my pain
and I found *joy* the next day...

...

Literal Lies

some people's lines are not meant to be read between; their words should be taken **literally** every time they speak. believe what they say in whatever way they say it. do not look for a way to make their **lies** seem *okay*.

...

I didn't realize my life had been on *pause*
until your love *stopped*
and I had to learn how to *play* each day
all alone on my **own**

...

·SOLILOQUIES & EPIPHANIES·

...

I am *numb* – but in a good way
I do not miss you; nor do I resent you
my heart is simply beginning to **forget** you

...

•SOLILOQUIES & EPIPHANIES•

...

I thought losing you was my greatest fear
I thought I would drown in my own tears
I thought I'd die a thousand times
as the pain ate me alive
but *when you left me*
the only thing I felt was **free**

...

Involuntary Forgiveness

I don't want to forgive you
I don't want to look forward
to growing from this lesson
I want to hate you
I want my contempt
to burrow into your soul
I want my pain to swallow us both
like a raging fire
I want my sorrows to burn in your lungs
as you drown in my tears
I want my misery to stab you in your heart
like the very knife you used to slice my love away

but my **grief** has already *faded away*
because hating you began to haunt me
and wishing pain upon you
only **plagued** my own heart

at times I wonder what we *could have been*
if we both weren't so stuck in our ways
if you weren't so **greedy**
and I wasn't so *giving*
if you didn't completely **ravish** my heart
and I didn't so willingly *relinquish* it

<u>-what if</u>

·SOLILOQUIES & EPIPHANIES·

...

one of these days
you're going to come *running back* to me
but I won't be there to comfort you
I will not be your **rebound** anymore
because I deserve more than someone
who only halfway loves me
when he's all out of options

...

•SOLILOQUIES & EPIPHANIES•

<u>*Note to Self*</u>

you are too forgiving; sometimes you might need to hold on to that **grudge** to help yourself *grow away* from those who mean you no good.

•SOLILOQUIES & EPIPHANIES•

...

I'm always too willing to *forgive others*
even when they show no remorse
for the pain they have caused me
but I can never seem to offer myself that same empathy
even though my wounds are healed
even though I've apologized to my reflection
even though I've promised to never hurt myself again
I still can't seem to **forgive myself** completely

...

4:50 in the afternoon

I need a minute
a minute to myself
a minute away from everyone else
from those I love
though I still love them
from those who hate
though the pain has not broken me
I need a minute to remember when to breathe
a minute to remember **me**
a minute to reminisce on how the world looked
when I viewed it through my own eyes
a minute to remember the sound of my own voice
a minute to relish in the vibrations of my heart
as it beats against my bones
a minute to *realign my soul*
I need a minute to myself
to remember **myself**

Tabernacle

after all my praying
God finally blessed me
now I'm free
free from your shackles
I found solace and safety in my own tabernacle
I am my own safe haven
no longer will I run to you when I need saving
I will run into my own arms
free from all harm
I let my tears fall into my own palms
I'm singing my own song
with words written in my own blood
that flowed from cuts
that I slit into my wrist
in a futile attempt
to free myself from you once before
but **no more** will I maim myself
or be shamed by the likes of you
someone who failed to see the *God in me*
and watched me cry on bended knees
ignored my pleas
disregarded my needs
gave me roses lined with thorns
just to watch me bleed
now I see
I see you for who you really are
geppetto with horns

·SOLILOQUIES & EPIPHANIES·

I was scarred by your scorn
pressed under your thumb
until my soul grew numb
I was dumb – to let you change who I was
I was dumb – to believe that this was true love
but **I'm done**
and *I will rise above*

...

...

I thought I would feel incomplete without you
I thought I would continuously yearn
for the pieces of me that you walked away with
but I do not need them
and **I do not need you**
because I have *rebuilt myself*
into someone completely new

...

•SOLILOQUIES & EPIPHANIES•

...

forgive me if I'm no longer the girl
you **broke** and took advantage of

forgive me for *walking away*
from your lies and **fake** love

forgive me for realizing
exactly what I am **worth**

forgive me as I **forgave** you
for causing me so much *hurt*

...

Finding Me

I tried so hard to be who you craved
that I *lost myself* along the way
a victim of your distaste
I barely recognized my own face

but I *walked away* from we
I stopped conforming to your needs
and in my search for she
I found the **me** I *used to be*

...

if I never let myself feel the *hurt*
my heart will never truly **heal**

...

•SOLILOQUIES & EPIPHANIES•

...

I found *beauty* in my **pain**

I *bathed* my body
in **rain**
that was meant to *drown* me

I *warmed* my skin
by **flames**
that tried to *burn* me

...

•SOLILOQUIES & EPIPHANIES•

a *spiritual coalescence* is taking place within my veins
I can feel the hands of **God** peeling my pain away

-baptized

Resurrection

I didn't think I'd be able to open up ever again
after you shut me out
but there are roses that **rebloom**
after they *die*
and the Sun still **lights** the sky
after every *dark night*
and so can I
just look within my eyes
all the tears that I cried
cleansed the pain I had inside
now I've come ***back to life***
more alive than last time

Reincarnation

you burned down my love
torched my heart
and left my soul melting
in flames of your own making
but I rose from the ashes
reforged and *recharged*
stronger and mightier
than ever before
you added fuel to a fire
in hopes to set me aflame
but it only **rekindled** my *self love*
now look how I shine
look how I glow
after growing from this pain
I will never again let you drag me
back down to your pits of hell

no longer putting all of my eggs in one basket
no longer giving *all of my love* to **one** person
even the sun shines its light
on more than one flower
no *one man* shall take all of my **power**

-spread love

•SOLILOQUIES & EPIPHANIES•

<u>*Why Me?*</u>

I like to think that there was something *special* about me
something *extraordinary* that drew you in

sparkles in my eyes

a melody in my laugh

sunshine in my smile

I like to think that you were **compelled** to love me
and that you didn't simply choose me on a whim

Oxygen ii

I don't need you to teach me how to breathe all on my own
I need you to *be my air*, so I won't gasp when I'm **alone**

...

I feel happy when I'm with him
the *same happiness* I felt with you
I'm just praying I don't go through
that **same pain** again too

...

Is This Real?

I know you have a past
I just hate the thought of you being affectionate
with anyone other than me
because your love feels rare
as if I've stumbled upon a hidden jewel
that no one else has ever come across
as if our hearts were dormant
until they met one another
but I know that isn't true
because I am not the only girl
who has been loved by you
and that is a reality that I cannot bare to face
and I'm not jealous nor am I angry
I just wish I could have been the first
your first
your one and only
but I'm not and I cannot help but wonder
if what we have is really real
because someone else already felt this same love
that I now feel

•SOLILOQUIES & EPIPHANIES•

I think I've found the other half of my heart in you
like puzzle pieces, we just fit
too much in common to simply be *coincidence*
this is *fate*; **kismet** if you will
I spent so many nights dreaming of you
and now you're real
and you are perfect
as if **God** created you *solely for me*
as if He told you to save your **soul** *only for me*

-meant to be

·SOLILOQUIES & EPIPHANIES·

I Want You

I don't want to start over with someone new
revealing my secrets to a stranger who
might not understand
I want you and only you
because no one else
can hold my heart in their hands
or undress my soul
or unzip my skin
or heal all the pain I have festering within
I have no problem letting you in
I welcome your touch
I crave your love
because you are everything
I have ever dreamed of
I don't want anyone else seeing
what your eyes have witnessed
or touching places your fingers
have already claimed as their own
or crossing lines that your lips have traced
to be face to face with anyone other than you
is a concept that my mind cannot comprehend
because **I want you and only you**
until the moment my life ends

·SOLILOQUIES & EPIPHANIES·

let's **heal** together
place your *broken* heart
in my *fractured* hands
help me remember who I am
let me show you who you were
as we **overcome** our hurt

-healing

·SOLILOQUIES & EPIPHANIES·

• ASCENSION •

·SOLILOQUIES & EPIPHANIES·

Finding Happiness

for so long I had been living **vicariously** through distant sunshine and foreign smiles, just imagining how that bliss must feel. but now I can taste that happiness on my own lips. *I see joy in my own eyes.* I finally found the rainbow that I had been chasing my whole life

Changing

I can feel myself **changing**
growing into who I was destined to be all along
no longer a victim of *past pain*
no longer drowning in heavy rains
I let these waters wash away my scars
I was led astray but I found my way
back into my own arms

...

falling for myself one flaw at a time
accepting my imperfections
until my heart and soul align

...

Loving Myself

I'm learning to love again
to **love myself** again
completely and unconditionally
not in spite of my scars
but because of them
because a rose cannot bloom
without rain
and you cannot heal
until you've outreigned pain

Alone Time

I've been spending some time on my own
not lonely, just **alone**
reconnecting with myself
rebuilding my soul
reclaiming my heart as my own
for so long, I had forgotten how to love me
I had forgotten how to be me
but this solitude has renewed my spirit
I can feel it in my bones
all my pieces are finally whole
I feel at home when I'm alone
I'm at peace when I'm on my own

Herstory

as I sat in silence
reflecting on my life
returning to myself
remembering my poems
I felt a longing for *who I once was*
a **yearning** for the girl *I used to be*
the girl whose soul is so intricately entangled
between these lines
within each verse
I find hidden gems of a heart that barely beats
but as I trace my fingers across these words
I can feel her pulse begin to quicken
she is coming back to me
with each page I turn
her presence becomes palpable
her spirit becomes tangible
like *braille to the blind*
every period and semicolon
fills my mind with the image of her smile
she is a novel with infinite chapters
and as I read on
I am **reunited** with my favorite story

•SOLILOQUIES & EPIPHANIES•

I've got words written on my skin
songs hidden within my flesh
stories that my eyes have only
just begun to see
and as I read,
I'm unlocking what it means
to be *me*
to be a *queen*
to be a **God**
despite my physical scars
every bruise is just a star
that illuminates the dark
and every lesion is a line
that holds a brand-new life

-discovering me

...

it takes a *special kind of entity* to be able to uplift those who have fallen so low; to heal those who have shattered beyond repair; to transform those who have lost themselves and **God**, I thank you every day in every way for being my saving grace

...

To Be A Woman

to be a woman – kissed by God
perfectly imperfect; flawlessly flawed
I am in awe of my own strength
so many burdens upon my hips
so much love within my soul
my eyes hold secrets I've never told
my voice sings of pleasure and pain
my heart brings lights to the darkest of days
my lips speak words that make angels applaud
because **I am a woman kissed by God**

Letter to Myself

I know you're trying to protect yourself by keeping your soul locked away from everyone else, but I'm here for you. I'm reaching out for your hands, but you've got your fists clenched tight, afraid that I might be out to break you like all the others. But we've grown into one another. *We are one.* Just look how your heart fills this hole in my chest. I was a shattered mess, but *you complete me*. You pieced me back together and **our rework** is so much more beautiful than my original. This is biblical love. The heavens above sent you straight to me and I know the angels must miss you because when I'm with you, we shine brighter than a thousand suns. The *lily of my valley*; my diamond in a dark alley. You healed all my pain. Stopped my eternal rain. Made my shadows run away. So, **I need you to stay.** I need your essence in my presence because without you, I'd crumble and stumble upon love that's been reduced to a mumble. But *our love is loud*, like a shout in the night. Doesn't it feel right when my skin is holding you tight? Flesh of my flesh, we've been bound for all eternity. You and I are the epitome of what love should truly be. So, you could never leave, for we are far too *entwined*. **I am yours and you are mine,** for every lifetime.

•SOLILOQUIES & EPIPHANIES•

Epiphany

there are diamonds in my soul
hidden beneath the coal
that you tried to bury me in
but I *searched deep within myself*
and **found the love** that no one else
was ever willing to offer
my hardened shell grew softer
I no longer need this suit of armor to protect me
for I've found the bravery I need to face the world
with open arms and an unlocked heart
my broken shards made whole
my secret scars now shown
I wear these *bruises* like **jewelry**
because you tried to ruin me
but I *overcame the pain*
and now there's nothing you could do to me
to ever make me falter
at times, I sit and ponder
on how I used to hide
the joy and bliss I had inside
like blowing out a candle
like flicking off a light
something deep within me died
and that's when you came alive
you thrived off my despair
and for a while I was unaware
until I got down on my knees
and asked **God** to *set me free*

•SOLILOQUIES & EPIPHANIES•

give me sight so I can see
that **I am all I'll ever need**
I heal my own wounds when I bleed
I rock my own soul to sleep
every missing piece I seek
is living right inside of me

...

•SOLILOQUIES & EPIPHANIES•

•SOLILOQUIES & EPIPHANIES•

<u>Special Thank You</u>

to my mother, *Da'vine*.
for being my rock
every time I crumbled...

•SOLILOQUIES & EPIPHANIES•

•SOLILOQUIES & EPIPHANIES•

for more follow me on social media

Instagram: @*al.vina.janae*
Twitter: @*alvina_janae*
YouTube: *al'vina janae*
SoundCloud: *al'vina janae*

Made in the USA
Columbia, SC
27 November 2018